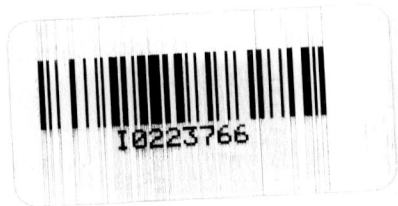

Seeds of Life

&

New Beginnings

Louise Ryan

Seeds of Life

&

New Beginnings

ACKNOWLEDGEMENTS

The people in my life who inspire me are my family and friends. I do not know where I would be without them. Thank you for supporting me throughout and giving me hope for another day. I have dedicated this book to my dad Phil. My dad passed away suddenly. He brought so much love, peace, humour, sunshine and his love of music to our lives. He will be forever missed. To my son Mikey and daughter Lily Beth, my stars, I love you both so much. You light up my life. To Richie, I want to thank you for all your support and belief in me. To my mum Patricia, I'm incredibly grateful to you for being there for me, especially when things were hard and I was hospitalised with my bipolar. To my sister Nick, you are not only my sister but my best friend. I'd be lost without you. Thanks for always listening to my work. To my brother Seán, I don't get to see you often but you inspire me to follow my dreams. To my niece and nephew Lauren and Jamie, whom I love very much. To my granny Elizabeth whom I cherish dearly. Thank you to John for all your support over the years. I'm very grateful to Laura for all your support, thank you for everything. To all my mum and Phil's family.

I want to thank my friends Brigid, Charleen, Declan, Dee, Jess, Sue and everyone who joined me on my Turas NLN journey. I love you all so much. To my childhood friends Dervla, Pamela, Rachel, Ruth and Vanessa, I'm so grateful for your support growing up and for being a part of my life. Thank you to all my mum's friends, especially Geraldine and Austin who were there for me since I was small. To Mike and family, although we've parted ways, thanks for being there for our children. To Ollie who has boosted my confidence in many ways through his humour and kind heart, thank you so much for everything. To all the NLN Mullingar staff. To all the staff at Threshold Training Network. To Michael Kenny, Camilla and all the staff at Maynooth University for all your support. To all the staff from AIT Athlone and Tullamore access course. Thank you for believing in me.

To Brian, the facilitator and co-founder of Inklings, thank you Brian for helping me to edit and self-publish my book. I am truly grateful. To my fellow Inkling Lorraine for reading my book and giving me feedback. Thank you so much. Lorraine has written a piece in my book in relation to the charity she co-founded called 'Our New Ears.' To my fellow Inkling Douglas who has hand-painted an amazing piece of artwork that is displayed in black and white in my book. To Samantha and Laurence for their dedication putting together a beautiful space for our work online: www.inklings.ie. To all my fellow Inklings, thank you for listening to my work, encouraging me and inspiring me to keep writing. To Donna who has written a piece in my book regarding a charity she set up in honour of her son Neil's memory called Neil's Hugs. Thank you from the bottom of my heart.

To my counsellor, thanks so much for being such a great support to me. To all my counsellors over the last number of years, I'm very grateful to you all. To Sarah from Shine, thanks so much to you and everyone from your organisation that helped me and my family when we needed help. Many teachers inspired me in school and as a mature student. Allen Carr has encouraged me to become myself, free from the nicotine trap. Hopefully I can help others through my poetry or through my book. To everyone that came into my life and changed it for the better. Thank you so much for everything. I thank God every day and am blessed in life to have such wonderful support around me. I love you all so much. So many charities and organisations have been so supportive to me and my family. I wish to thank them all. The St. Vincent de Paul has been a massive help to my family when things were difficult. To all the special people who were a part of our life that are no longer with us. They are all heroes to me.

Everyone is constantly learning no matter what age they are. Every day is a learning process. It is my passion to write more books in the future. I love writing and sharing my work with people. I want to make a difference in people's lives. To all the readers of my work, I thank you dearly.

Dad Phil

Dear Dad, I love you to the moon and back and more,
I'll miss you forever, my heart is torn,
you were an incredible man so gentle, warm and kind,
a smile you brought to many, your generosity was
inspired.

You and Mum were like two peas in a pod,
you had a strong faith and love for God,
you loved playing the drums in the church band,
you loved the beach, walking on the sand.

Dad, you loved Wicklow since you were just a boy,
you loved fishing and chess, you were a genuine guy,
you had a love for animals- cats, dogs and more,
you had a hearty laugh that would make others smile for
sure.

Dad, you were my hero and my hero you'll always be,
the best Dad I could ever ask for, your smile I'll always
see,
you cheered up anyone who walked your way,
you're with God now, in our hearts you'll forever stay.

Love from your daughter xxx

Artwork by Douglas Raeside

CONTENTS

INTRODUCTION

'It starts with a dream, Add faith, and it becomes a belief,
Add action, and it becomes a part of life, Add
perseverance, and it becomes a goal in sight, Add
patience and time, and it ends with a dream come true'
(**Doe Zantamata**)

Life's Rollercoaster

Life can be amazing, a roller coaster of beautiful
miracles,
we get stronger through the many challenging obstacles,
see the beauty in the world around,
no stone left unturned, no unexplored ground.

There can be joy found in all we do,
we've just got to keep active and plodding through,
talk to someone close when you're feeling blue,
better out than in, then our problems will be few.

Life can be a precious package, wrapped tight, filled with
delight,
bringing hope, meaning and waves of light,
let your intuition set you free, within the imagination-
who believes?
hope and love lead the way to the magic of your dreams.

Trust in your inner instinct, hope is closer than you think,
don't be afraid to be distinct, life can go by in a blink,
follow your inner guidance, follow your heart,
it may just be a good thing if you've to go back to the
start.

I love reading quotes, so I've decided to start each chapter with a quote and I've tried to relate each poem I've written to each chapter. I wrote the following quote a few years ago. 'Aim for the stars and if you don't reach them yet you can enjoy all the fluffy clouds that might just take you to a rainbow of different opportunities.' Every path you take in life leads you to another and even though you may not like the track you are on, you will find one thing - strength. You may not see this now but the 'difficult roads often lead to beautiful destinations.' (Author Unknown)

I suffered with anxiety and depression since I was a child. At the age of 26 I found out I had been diagnosed with bipolar disorder. I've had five hospitalisations from the age of twenty-one up until I was thirty-nine lasting an average of three months each time, except for the last admission in 2022 which was for five weeks and five days.

I started my first job around the age of fourteen delivering newspapers and had many different jobs over ten years. I have worked in many professions including care assisting, waitressing and sales. I have management experience and have worked in office administration also. I fell ill in 2007 and was hospitalised when my first child was merely four weeks old. I was introduced to a book around that time by an old friend that changed my life in a very positive way. 'The Secret' by Rhonda Byrne.

I decided to return to education after building up my confidence and unlocking 'the secret.' I began thinking positively, practicing gratitude, goal setting and visualisation. I commenced the Access 21 further education course but became ill with anxiety and psychosis and was hospitalised and restarted it the following year. I successfully completed it and then in 2013 went on to pursue my degree in Front Office and Tourism Management and in 2014 I graduated with an honours degree in Tourism and Hospitality Management.

I had always wanted to teach since a young age and in 2015 an opportunity presented itself to start a teaching course in further education. I became ill during the course and was hospitalised again when my youngest child was only ten months old. I experienced high episodes this time. The hardest time of my life was being away from my family. I attended a literacy tutor training course and completed it in 2017. The same year I restarted the Higher Diploma in Further Education and graduated in 2018. I am delighted to have completed a two-year course in personal development that relates to wellness. I completed a two-year retail course. I recently completed the TEFL course, teaching English as a foreign language. I have been studying over the last 15 years and enjoyed every moment of it.

I am a proud mum of two, both who never cease to amaze and inspire me. I enjoyed volunteering as an IT tutor and helping out assisting the coaches with the disability tag rugby team. I get involved in various mental health groups and feel my health has been restored through the support of family and friends, attending courses, reading and listening to many self-help books, practicing affirmations, changing my thought patterns and having faith in life. I have been a part of Inklings writers' group over the past eight years and have enjoyed taking part in the women's mini marathon over the past number of years. I am chuffed to have quit smoking again.

I feel I have been on a journey of self-empowerment, personal growth, self-transformation, inner-peace and hope. I have found that there is always hope, even when you are in a dark hole but you will discover your own silver lining of prosperity and walk right through. I started writing this book in and around 2008 shortly after watching 'The Secret' documentary. I believed in myself. I put my book on the back burner while I returned to education but I tapped away at it over the years. If this book helps at least one person then I am happy.

CHAPTER 1: THE BEST THINGS IN LIFE ARE FREE

'The two most important days in your life are the day you are born and the day you find out why'
Mark Twain

A Splash of Life

Whispering waves, beneath they fall
into a fascinating world, a wonder-wall,
if I danced like the ocean and dreamt like the skies,
submerged precious and pure is what truly lies,
a tranquil treasure, we know so deep and blue,
a reflection of our hearts, so free and true,
miles and miles of uncovered beauty and depth,
a secret, an essence, a presence to be kept,
a splash of life that unearths your soul,
a majestic ocean, a sand patrol,
seashell seashell on the seashore,
seashell, a seashell,
discovers a bellowing for more.

My family are my world. Living with an illness makes life even more precious than before I was diagnosed with bipolar. I try not to take things as much for granted. I am grateful for every day I have on this earth to tell and show those dear to me that I love them. I try to take each day and moment as it comes. 'The best kind of people are the ones that come into your life, and make you see the sun where you once saw clouds. The people that believe in you so much you start to believe in you too. The people that love you, simply for being you. The once in a lifetime kind of people.' (Author Unknown)

CHAPTER 2: YES I CAN IS STEP ONE IN YOUR LIFE PLAN

'If you can dream it then you can do it'
Walt Disney

Yes I Can

Yes I can is step one in your life plan,
believe in yourself and that you can,
write it down, keeping it to hand,
make that change, take that stand.

Believe in yourself, I can't stress it enough,
life can be hard, the challenges tough,
get out of your comfort zone, bear through the rough,
think of what keeps you going and those you love.

Never doubt your power within,
today is the first day of your life to begin,
never give up, just take things day by day,
after all, life is only a short stay.

So replay those positive thoughts over in your mind,
in doing this over and over you will find,
there's no room for negativity just thoughts that are kind,
start a blank canvas, your goals redefined.

Yes I can... Self-belief is having trust in your own abilities. If you don't have trust in yourself how can anybody else trust in you? If you don't believe you can do something then you will find it harder to complete that goal. Have you ever said to yourself: 'I can't... and then what happens... you can't. Well, try telling yourself in your mind or shout it out if you like and say 'I can!' Things will start to have a knock-on positive effect and good things just might start to happen in your life. 'The biggest wall you've got to climb is the one you build in your mind.' (Roy T Bennett) 'I can't' is surrounded by negativity and in turn negativity is what will magnetise. Writing things down and leaving it where you can see it helps you focus on what it is you want in life. This is my belief because it is something I have done over the past number of years. It's like it's etching it in your mind and helps you to keep on track.

Write down everything that you thought you couldn't do that you want to do in the form of 'I can', for example 'I can stop smoking.' Write down step by step guidelines looking at how you are going to achieve the goal or tips that will help you succeed. For instance, if it is smoking you wanted to quit you could write down: I will listen to Allen Carr's audio for an hour a day, I will keep a bottle of water with me all the time, I will have the reasons I want to quit in my pocket or in my bag or close to me. These mini goals will help bring us closer to our goals and remind us why we wanted to get there in the first place.

The WHY of your goals is important. Ask yourself that question. Why do I wish to achieve this goal? What will I get out of it? What will it bring me? Why is it so important to me? Writing down the 'whys' of your goal can ignite the passion behind your goal and allow you to become closer to it. For instance, if you want to go to a particular place with your family on holiday, the 'whys' of this goal might be: more family time together, unwind and revitalise my mind, body and soul, a chance to explore different places or return to familiar territory, learn some words of a new language, it is exciting meeting new people, experiencing different cultures, having fun and more. The more 'whys' you have on your list the stronger the flame will be and it will spark you in the right direction.

Another question you could ask yourself is: who else will benefit from you achieving this goal? The more people that it will benefit, the stronger the driving force will be behind it.

CHAPTER 3: HAVE THE FAITH - BE IN A PEACEFUL STATE

'Surrender to what is, let go of what was, have faith in what will be'
Ricotti

Thank You God

Thank you God for finding me when I was alone and lost,
it is you Lord God that I searched for and after you I sought,
when I'm afraid you soothe me and wrap me in your golden cloth,
your light I have found, your love I have caught.

Lord God I know you always help us and guide us through the day,
thank you for my loved ones, for their safety I always pray,
for everything I have, for keeping negativity at bay,
for every day I have and for taking my worries away.

So, I pray Lord God for a healthy, happy life for those I love so dear,
for my little sweet-hearts I try my best to rear,
for all those who are a part of my life and make my life so clear,
I pray for everyone, far and near.

'Maybe it's not that easy, but maybe it's not that difficult either. Every moment is possible. Moments become days and days become years. Looking back you'll wonder how you made it through an impossible time. You'll have done it moment by precious, possible moment.' (Doe Zantamata) I have a strong faith in God. I have had some experiences where I felt very close to God and Our Lady. I was twenty-one when I was hospitalised for the first time. I wasn't eating much, talking, sleeping or taking care of myself. I wasn't there in many ways, like an empty shell. Twenty-one is a lucky number for me. I turned to God and I feel God helped me to get through one of the hardest times of my life. It is the 'key to the door' as they say and I hope if you find one thing from this book it is to help you unlock your own door of opportunity in life and walk right through.

When my faith was restored, it helped me through a lot. I began to see positive change in my life when I turned to God. When I started believing again I felt the warmth of the sun on my face and I felt a strong presence of God. I felt all my worries leave my body, I felt inner peace, I felt at one with myself, a feeling I had never felt before. God can give us peace of mind if we ask for help. Peace of mind is something we all wish for and it is there for us if we just ask, see it in our minds, feel it already in our hearts and truly believe we can have it. It's difficult to journey along a straight road twenty-four seven. The road is always bendy. The twists and turns in the road allow us to achieve challenges and feel the rewards after we overcome those barriers and unlock our true strength. Some setbacks in life make us come out stronger on the other side, although we may not see it at the time. 'God is thinking about you right at this moment even if you feel forgotten by people, God will never forget you, he loves you that much' (On Wings of Hope Facebook Page)

CHAPTER 4: BEAT YOUR DISORDER AND PURSUE YOUR GOALS FURTHER

'Sometimes it takes an overwhelming breakdown to have an undeniable breakthrough'
Unknown

See the Signs

See the signs, track them early,
take your meds, not only rarely,
love yourself, treat yourself fairly,
life is how you see it, try not to see it as scary.

Be yourself, not just your illness,
meditate into a world of stillness,
if we think good then it will bring this,
things don't have to be full of grimness.

Listen to your favourite track,
live, laugh, love, have the craic,
say goodbye to that panic attack
and cut yourself a big piece of slack.

Free yourself of that mind pain,
see life as good, you've so much to gain,
count all your blessings at the end of the day,
read, write, rest and dream big as you lay.

Having a mental illness used to have a stigma attached to it and I feel it still does in some ways but not as much. There's so much more awareness of mental health nowadays but we've a long way to go. A very strong, inspirational woman once told me this quote and it makes a lot of sense to me. 'Those who mind don't matter and those who matter don't mind.' It took me many years not to care what strangers thought of me and now I just try my best to only care about what my family and close friends think. I wrote 'I try my best' for the very reason that it is hard to block out negativity from others no matter how hard you try.

My stress levels have reduced because I'm not listening to negativity from others. Many people in the world suffer from depression and those who get high or manic as well as depressed can be diagnosed with bipolar disorder. On the bipolar scale for me the downs outweighed the highs

Most people will be affected by mental health at some point in their life. It can either affect themselves or a family member, a loved one, a friend or someone they know. There needs to be more awareness raised so those affected know they aren't alone and are able to seek help before it gets worse.

I know stress was a big factor in my life and not being able to deal with it caused me to end up where I was, helpless and needed others to take over. It is not shameful to do this and many people throughout life will go through something in their lives where they cannot cope and need help along the way. We can all just be there for others, try to notice the signs and talk to the person that may be affected or ask them to talk to a professional. I have attended many therapy sessions over the years and it's difficult to say 'I need help' and get the assistance you need. The Samaritans do great work and provide a 24hr service: 116 123 is a free number for those who need help. I've rang the Samaritans before and they were brilliant. Sometimes you cannot speak to family or friends. The Samaritans are there to help. A smile or kind word can go a long way in someone's life. If you can't think of a compliment to say to another person then say nothing.

What can you do for yourself living with bipolar or other mental health illnesses? How can you avoid getting unwell again? Try and look out for signs, watch out for more negative and racing thoughts. Talk to those you care about; can they see a difference in you? Every chapter I've written, I've tried to link to wellness in some form or another. I feel well most days. I try to think positive, thinking of those I love. I look at my vision board, all of the things I'd love to do. I love spending time with those I love or talking to them on the phone. I make time for being creative like playing guitar, writing a poem or writing this book.

Writing is a good way of expressing how you feel and getting it out rather than letting thoughts weigh you down. I would recommend you start writing as a way of therapeutic de-stressing even if it's just writing down daily or weekly goals. When you get them down on paper it does make you feel that bit better within yourself. Writing down your worries is another way to release stress. When they're on paper they don't seem as intimidating. You could write down something positive that may come from your problem. You can then throw all your worries away. I love attending Inklings writing group where my worries usually disappear for a few hours while I escape into a different world.

Getting involved in as many groups as possible helped my wellness. I enjoyed doing kickboxing many years ago and then I started boxercise as a hobby for a bit. It helped me to relieve stress. There are many groups I took part in, some of them really helped my mental health. I thoroughly enjoyed the soccer, tag rugby, boxercise, scrapbooking class, Zumba and WRAP (Wellness Recovery Action Programme). They give you the feel-good factor, releasing stress and building up your self-esteem. Going to the gym also allowed me to do this as well. Slimming world helped me to make lots of healthy changes and I intend to make more. I still attend Inklings. I look forward to it every week and it helps with my mental health.

Tips that kept me well

- Keeping active is a way of staying well.
- Spend time with loved ones who support you and avoid people who don't.
- Take your medication.
- Talk to a professional about problems you are having. An illness doesn't have to prevent you from pursuing your dreams.
- If you feel yourself slipping, ask your doctor to review your medication.
- Read books that you connect with or if you haven't got the concentration or would prefer listening to them instead then go for it.
- Do stretches.
- Listen to relaxation music.
- Think you are well and you will start to feel well.
- Take deep breaths - inhale the good thoughts, exhale the bad thoughts.
- Put an ice pack on the back of your neck for racing thoughts.
- Try to get a balanced sleep and diet. (That's easier said than done.)

Sleep deprivation was a big factor to my diagnosis.

I was stressed out, not getting enough sleep and the less sleep I got the more worried I was. I feel anything natural that enhances sleep will be good such as relaxation music, exercise, reading a 'can't put you down' book, aromatherapy oils, whatever works, try it. It might just be the wellness factor of your wellbeing.

Look out for signs of slipping, if you see them then tell someone, including your doctor. When I was ill I found there were a lot of supports around me. I was given a contact for community mums and the lady called to me for a chat. They help families around different locations that have babies and young children. A social worker met with us to help with different matters that were prominent at the time. She helped me with financial matters and other issues that needed dealing with. She pointed us in the right direction and gave us different contact names and numbers. The occupational therapists ran different groups that I enjoyed attending. I took part in different mental health groups. The Decider Skills and the Eolas Mental

Health course were two different group courses available to sign up to. The Decider Skills really exceeded my expectations. There are so many skills to help deal with mental health, I still use many skills today. One of the skills that I use when I'm feeling anxiety coming on or when I'm in a queue is the 54321 skill. **Five** things you can see. **Four** things you can touch. **Three** things you can hear. **Two** things you can taste or smell and just take **One** deep breath. There were many role-plays throughout the Decider Skills Course that allowed you to see things clearer in each different scenario. These courses helped me to understand my illness better and see that I was not alone.

CHAPTER 5: KNOW YOU WILL BENEFIT AND IT'S EASIER TO QUIT

'It always seems impossible until it's done'
Nelson Mandela

Now I am free

Set a date and quit the smoke,
be your own hero it's no joke,
say goodbye and stab out that yoke,
no more being absolutely stone broke.
Feel the goodness of the fresh air we breathe,
be confident in knowing from the trap we are freed,
to take one step at a time is all we need,
to know we can do it if we plant the 'I CAN' seed.
So, if we slip up, we dust off and start again,
we re-evaluate why we want to quit,
putting paper to pen,
have faith in ourselves and encourage each other when,
we are having a bad day now and then.

I was caged for many years, I smoked when facing fears,
caught inside the nicotine trap-I puffed to fill that gap.
Allen Carr helped me to stop
and still helps many make their habit hop,
though he has passed this life,
with his clinics worldwide and his books alike.
His method seems to work,
to stop the 'nicotine monster' lurk,
it's called 'the Easyway', I take it day by day.

Now I am free

They caused me to cough and splutter,
'they're killing me' I would mutter
but yet I would still puff away,
inside the trap I was a slave.
They made my teeth and nails stained,
many times from smoking I refrained
but the smoking net caught me again
many times I'd tried, I'd say at least ten.
I attempted the herbal smokes and the patches
but I'd feel the fear of needing cigs and matches,
I trusted in myself and gave it my best,
now I am free I guess, now I am put to the test.

I am now able to walk and jog
without being out of breath,
the money for smokes was piling up my debt,
I completed a marathon
something I never thought I'd do,
I started the gym and walking most days too.
I feel less stressed now I'm not smoking,
I feel healthier and no longer coughing and choking,
I can do more of what I enjoy that's for sure,
like writing, playing guitar, crocheting and more.
I feel like I have a second chance in life every day,
I'm off them now, hopefully that's the way it will stay,
to the nicotine monster I no longer belong,
now I am free, I've got to stay strong!

'Since 1983 Allen Carr's Easyway to Stop Smoking method has helped millions of smokers quit smoking and find freedom from cigarettes.' (www.allencarr.com) Some smokers have a fear that if they quit smoking they won't be able to deal with stresses that life can throw at them. Well, yes, they can cope even better because smoking actually causes stress in peoples' lives. Think of a situation where you have no cigarettes left, the stress it causes. If you are a non-smoker, you will have lots less to worry about. Sometime before I quit smoking in 2005 I wrote a list of why I wanted to quit and before I knew it, I had a bundle of reasons why I wanted to quit, more reasons than why I wanted to smoke. They stayed with me on my smoke-free journey. I was smoke free for six years and eight months. I am now off the cigarettes three years, since my last hospital admission in 2022.

The one reason I wanted to smoke was because of fear of not being able to stop. There is no fear in quitting if you read Allen Carr's book as it leaves an imprint in your head of how easy it can be to quit and gives you the guidance you need to help you along the way. He has written different books on this, and there is also a PC disk and clinics all around the world as well. I am glad I came across his books as I've tried chewing gum, herbal cigarettes and none of them worked. I had hypnosis once and I think that helped too.

Allen Carr's books are somewhat hypnotic as well where they really get into your mindset and change your beliefs about smoking to make a positive impact on you. I truly believe it is mind over matter and if you think you can do it then you will. I don't have many cravings. Hopefully, I'll stay off them. The best thing to do if you do have one slip is to remember you don't have to go back on the cigarettes. Say to yourself: I AM STILL A NON-SMOKER.

Tips that helped me to quit

- Read Allen Carr's books.
- Listen to his audio book.
- Avoid alcohol for a while if you are used to smoking while drinking.
- Keep a bottle of water with a squeeze of lemon juice with you, taking sips if you feel anxious.
- Make a list of why you want to quit and the benefits.
- Keep a pack of sugar free mints handy.
- Learn how to knit or crochet.
- Deep breaths, enjoy breathing in fresh air, feel the deep breath inhaling all the goodness and as you exhale imagine any of the ill effects of smoking blowing away.

Benefits of Quitting

- You'll have a healthier mind and body.
- You will save money, approximately (20 a day for 1 year is an average of €16 x 7 days x 52 weeks = €5824 savings a year).
- You will become fitter and healthier.
- There will be a fresher scent on your clothes, breath, hair, etc.
- You will enjoy the taste of food again.
- Your nails will grow back the colour they are supposed to be.
- You can enjoy the fresh air.
- You will enjoy a less stressful environment - smoking actually causes stress.
- You will have less worries - smoking involves constant worrying of when you need to get your next packet.
- You are leading by example to your children and loved ones.
- There is less panic - the panic you feel when you run out or you lose them.
- You have less hangovers - I haven't felt a bad hangover since I quit smoking. Some people I've talked to feel the same.
- There is constant panic when forbidden to have a cigarette in different locations - cinemas, pubs trains, buses etc.
- There is less worry about your health.
- You are free of the trap…

THE NICOTINE TRAP!

CHAPTER 6: WITH A DECENT NIGHT'S REST YOU'LL BE AT YOUR BEST

'Let her sleep for when she wakes she will move mountains'
Shakespeare

Sleep is the Answer

Sleep is everything, it's second to none,
to rest and get a proper sleep is easier said than done,
you can put certain oils on your pillowcase,
even wear a night mask on your face.
You can read and unwind,
think positive in your mind,
there's meditation, you could try a body scan,
the following day you could pre-plan.
Listen to music if that helps,
declutter your room, reorganise those shelves,
write down your worries in a notebook,
counting sheep you should not overlook.
Himalayan salt lamps can be used to help you sleep,
you'll be worn out if you exercise a few times a week,
drink some hot chocolate or warm milk,
while in bed try not to overthink.
Try your best to get a proper rest,
with some decent shut-eye you'll be at your best,
think of all your favourite happenings over the day,
let your mind wander to nothing as you lay.

A proper night's sleep is imperative. There's definitely a thin line between wellness and illness when you don't get the sleep your body needs. You can use aids to help you sleep like relaxation music, body scan meditations, oils and herbal remedies.

Often you can be kept awake because of worries so if you write down what's bothering you or talk it out with a family member or friend you will feel much lighter and it might just be the difference in getting sleep and not getting enough. Lack of sleep can cause you to worry more than you need to and can make small problems seem bigger, massive even. If napping during the day limit it to less than an hour and try not to nap after five pm, it will prevent you from sleeping at night unless you are doing night shifts and that's your routine.

Tips on sleeping better

- Try to get into a pattern of going to sleep at the same time most nights.
- Keep the room as dark as possible.
- Turn off sound on devices one hour before bed.
- Try meditation.
- Limit your caffeine intake, even tea too close to bedtime can keep you awake.
- Listening to relaxing music may help.
- Put certain aromatherapy oils like lavender on your pillowcase.
- Have a hot shower or bath before bed.
- Fill a hot water bottle in winter.

CHAPTER 7: ADDRESS AND MANAGE THAT STRESS

S.T.R.E.S.S: '*Someone Trying to Repair Every Situation Solo*'

David Willis

Stress

Managing stress will help you stay at your best,
focus on those supporting you, avoid the rest,
try to get walking and eat the right food,
it's amazing how much they can alter your mood.
I've mentioned before about getting enough sleep,
it's also important not to stress about those deadlines
you've to meet,
you'll get things done if you take them one step at a time,
trust in God and everything will be just fine.
On your journey there will always be a twist or a bend,
grab life by the reins, you'll get there in the end,
share your burdens with someone close,
practice being thankful for who and what you love most.
Go to your happy place, it could be a beach, a lake or
anywhere,
live life every day without a care,
have a cuppa if you're feeling stressed,
think about how in life you are blessed.

If you stress too much about something before it happens, you basically put yourself through it twice.' (Unknown Author) It's good to talk things out with your family, close friends or a professional counsellor. Sometimes a problem seems massive inside but once you get it out it doesn't seem as big. It is imperative to get enough sleep to maintain wellness. Diet is important in wellness. Sugary foods or drinks that are high in caffeine can prevent you from getting a proper sleep. If you are not getting enough nutrition, your body can stop functioning properly. It is necessary to have a balanced diet. Your diet can be linked to wellness as well. Try and get as much fresh air as you can. The Fitbit or step counters are a great idea as they encourage you to get your steps in. If you set up your day the night before you'll be less stressed. Write a few lines of what you would like to achieve the following day. Give yourself that me-time. It is important to have that time for yourself. Run that Radox bath, listen to relaxation music, read your favourite book or just unwind doing your favourite thing. Sometimes my words can be repetitive but I am just trying to stress the importance of the different wellness tips. I hope it helps. I find it's good to talk out how you are feeling but if you put all your energy into talking about illness then it may contribute to you feeling ill. Talk about wellness, talk about everything you can do to make yourself feel better.

CHAPTER 8: CREATIVITY INCREASES POSITIVITY

*'Music gives a soul to the universe, wings to the mind,
flight to the imagination and life to everything'*
Plato

Creativity Increases Positivity

Creativity keeps you on your toes,
it unlocks your true potential and it shows
that nothing is difficult, into the possible it goes,
it brings passion to your life, lifting your lows.

Creativity can run from activities to sports,
it's healing that hurt and soothing those thoughts,
it can be therapeutic, bringing fun to lots,
creativeness can help you find yourself when all else feels
lost.

Creativity increases positivity, it's great for your
wellbeing,
dance, play an instrument, take photographs sightseeing,
make a vision board or a scrapbook of all your favourite
stuff,
sketch, join a club, taking up knitting or crocheting may
lift you right up.

Gardening, cooking, painting the house are all creative
things to do,
from woodwork to sewing to name but a few,
give it a shot, what have you got to lose,
there are many different things you can choose.

Finding something you enjoy doing,
giving you a focus, can prevent you stewing
or getting anxious or unwell,
it may bring you right out of your panic filled shell.

Idea generation and using your hands is good for the mind,
being creative allows you that well deserved 'me time',
creativity relaxes you and helps you unwind,
create your own masterpiece, a path to your passion you
will find.

Every day say to yourself, I will do at least one thing that is creative. Anything from sketching or painting a picture to writing a poem, a short story or a chapter for your own book. Sing, dance, play an instrument or take part in a yoga class. Start a pottery class, capture beautiful photographs, do a spot of gardening, learn embroidery and make your own masterpiece. These are all soothing for the mind and can reduce stress and negativity in your life. It encourages self-expression allowing you to get to know yourself that bit better.

I enjoy writing, writing poems, writing goals, writing this book, it allows me to express myself better. I enjoy playing guitar, something I have yet to master! I love playing board games with my kids - scrabble, chess, cards and many more. Creating vision boards, taking photos and sketching are different things I like to do to help keep me well. I attended writing, art and guitar classes all of which I thoroughly enjoyed.

CHAPTER 9: BEING POSITIVE IS A MAGICAL CAUSATIVE

'We are all in the gutter but some of us are looking at the stars'
Oscar Wilde

Positivity

Being positive opens up a new world for you,
things seem easier to clasp when they're in your view,
when you visualise and picture getting what you need
and give thanks for all, things will sprout from that seed.

Miracles can happen with just one word, hope,
without it I don't think I could cope,
it keeps me believing in the unknown,
there's always hope even when you think you're all alone.

So try picturing your day going well before it starts happening,
the thoughts are like presents you're unwrapping,
send a smile someone's way,
positivity is contagious, you might just make their day!

'When you smile, even when you don't feel like it, you are opening the pathway to your heart…And once the pathway is opened the next smile comes easier. That's why smiles are contagious and instantly connect people heart to heart.' (Begin with Yes Facebook Page) If you think positive then things will start to happen for the better, as mentioned in Rhonda Byrne's 'The Secret' magic started to happen to me after reading the book. Your belief in yourself and others is stronger and this starts to rub off on you and those around you and before you know it you are starting a positive, contagious, knock on effect. If you start to think superstitiously on Friday the thirteenth, for instance, then as soon as one bad thing happens it leads to more negative happenings and before you know it all the bad events happened just because you were expecting them. Expect good things in your life, you deserve to give yourself the biggest chance in life that you can give. Stay around people who uplift you and avoid those who don't. Stay positive, a positive mind is a healthy one. Thinking one positive thought can retrieve you from a black hole. One positive thought can change your life for the better.

Don't let your emotions take over. If you feel bad then you know you are thinking about negative things. Try to be aware of how you feel so you can deal with replacing those bad feelings with feel good factors. Being positive says no to depression. Positivity doesn't allow negative thoughts or situations come to light. Continually thinking good thoughts will make you feel happier. This can be hard at the start, especially if you were used to criticism by others growing up, like me. It is a hard pattern to break because the negativity stays with you as you get older. It's a hard nut to crack. It's like you have to try and retrain your brain. When you hear that inner voice putting you down, try and catch that thought and ask yourself why you think that thought. You may find it was something that you were frequently told as a child. You could say to yourself, I don't deserve to be treated this way. I am now deciding to treat myself better and talk to myself in a kinder manner.

Write a list of your good qualities, achievements and strengths. This can bring your mind into a better state of self-esteem. It is harder to think good thoughts when you're thinking bad of yourself. Thinking of your good qualities, achievements and strengths will put you in a more positive frame of mind. Think of the achievements you are trying to conquer as well. Imagine they are already with you and they will be. Reading books based on true stories can be helpful, where you can associate with another person that has been through similar situations. If there is someone out there who has gone through a similar experience, you can feel for that person, empathise with them and know that you are not alone.

Accept yourself: Self-acceptance is key and you'll feel more positive within. I came across the following quote by Mark Sterling. 'If you want to soar in life, you must first learn to FLY- First Love Yourself.' It is hard for some people to accept themselves because they hadn't felt accepted their whole lives or felt they didn't fit in. If you felt rejected as a child it is harder to accept yourself. Accepting myself as me was a hard task especially since I didn't really know who I was. I felt rejected by many people as a child. I now accept myself fully as a person who deserves happiness but this took a long time. It is hard to accept yourself fully. I am learning now to love myself, something I couldn't do before. I listen to Marisa Peer's meditations often. She talks about how you need to tell yourself 'I AM ENOUGH.' She suggests writing it down and to put it somewhere you can see every day. Shine is an organisation that promotes wellness, a service I have availed of when I was unwell. They do amazing work. There are many more organisations that I have not mentioned but I know they are doing great work to help others who suffer with ill mental health and this puts hope into my world and I'm sure many others' world too.

Positivity reduces stress in your life but negativity causes worry and anxiety which leads to stress. Look at photos, pictures and quotes that make you smile. They remind you that there are people in life who care and you can reminisce on many happy times. A reminder of a happy time can bring many positive thoughts to light and evaporate any not so good thoughts. Share positivity with others encouraging them and supporting them. Passing on the positivity will not only make the other person feel good but you'll feel good knowing you've helped someone else. My wish is to help others every day even if it is just a smile that goes their way, a smile can make a difference to someone's life.

If you can act positive you are halfway there. Acting positive creates a feel-good feeling in your body and in turn you will receive positive feelings. So, even if you are having a bad day then know that you can change it at the click of a finger. Realistically it may not be as simple as that but it can happen shortly afterwards. Being optimistic is expecting good things to happen and they will happen if you believe it and stay optimistic. Reading positive quotes and stories helped uplift me when I felt down.

Show appreciation and gratitude. Being thankful in life is something we all at one point in our lives can forget to do. Let those you love know how much you are thankful to them or show them that you care. Be aware of the present moment. This allows you to see where you are now and where you want to be in the future. Smile more, smiling is definitely contagious. Smiling is great and it's free. It's one of the best things in life as you can truly change your mood or somebody else's just by smiling. I can take life too seriously at times but it's good to remind yourself to laugh.

Relax, do yoga, sing, dance anything that helps you to unwind. Give yourself a makeover or exchange makeovers with friends or get a sample in the shop. The grass on the other side is NOT greener. Envy is a disastrous path to destruction. The less of it you have the better off you are. Rid yourself of envy forever. Stop comparing your life to others. Everyone's journey has a different pace. Talk to inspirational people. They will eventually rub off on you and before you know it you will be reaping the benefits of their influence. Don't blame yourself or others. Blame leads to pity, pity to low self-worth and low self-worth, well, it's a black hole we don't want to be in. Let go of blame for yourself and for others. It's a worthless cause. Be healthier, exercise and eat healthy. I started a positive jar for the last number of years. You can write down all of the good things that happened to you each day or each week and on New Year's Eve you can look through all the great things that occurred throughout the year. You can even pick a random note out of the jar on a day you're feeling down. You could then put them in a scrapbook. It allows you to focus on the positive aspects of your life.

Is there anyone in your life that constantly sees the negative in life? If so, it might be an idea to tell them that they seem to be somewhat negative. They may not have even been aware of it. If they continue to be negative it might be an option to keep your distance from that person. Though it may not be intentional, they can bring you down and before you know it you'll be seeing the negative in people and talking negatively. It's a different situation if someone is going through a difficult time, of course things may be negative for some time. I'm talking about people who complain all the time, where they have so much to be grateful for but they cannot see it. They can talk about others in envy, they can gossip endlessly. It's a downward negative spiral that can blow out of control and it seems that you can attract negative happenings into your life because of this. Here's a little thing you can do: Every time you notice you are making a negative comment about yourself or others then you can make five compliments about yourself or others instead.

CHAPTER 10: GRATITUDE IS THE RIGHT KIND OF ATTITUDE

'Yesterday is history, tomorrow is a mystery and today is a gift which is why we call it the present'
Alice Morse Earle

Gratitude

Gratitude is the right kind of attitude,
many times my faith has been renewed,
I pray to God and thank God for life,
I feel like God is with me through the strife.

I think of everything I'm grateful for-
my family, friends and so much more,
I take every day as it comes,
every time I get to inhale from my lungs.

Bring a gratitude stone wherever you go,
when you feel it in your hands you'll know,
it will remind you of who and what you're grateful for,
so pick a special one to be sure.

Focus on blessings instead of complaints,
give thanks to God and all the angels and saints,
we are given a second chance in life each day,
I'm over the moon I'm here today.

Gratitude is the right kind of attitude to have and to live by, giving thanks for all we have. One can use a gratitude rock, start now don't be shy. I'm so lucky to be here today with my family and loved ones. I try not to focus on all the bad that has happened but I think of all the good I have in my life. I wanted to write this book to encourage others to reach for their dreams. Just because you have an illness does not mean you cannot do something you really want to do. There were times I wanted to give up but I kept just taking things one day at a time and taking it step by step. There is always a way to do what you are passionate about. I am very grateful to those who helped me to get here. I am thankful to so many people that have been a part of my life. You all know who you are. Those that I have had the pleasure of meeting along my journey, I am forever grateful.

Did you ever find yourself complaining about what you have and all of a sudden you get more to complain about. 'The Secret' reveals that this is the law of attraction in action, like attracting like. I love the idea about the gratitude rock in 'The Secret'. It can be a rock, bead or even clove of garlic if you like. Keep it close to you, in your bag or your pocket as it's something to inspire grateful thoughts and feelings. I am getting into the routine of practicing gratitude every day that I wake up. I say it when I take my first steps out of bed. I watch my slideshow of gratitude. Life can take over and when you are in the flow of life you can forget to be thankful. I keep a stone in my purse to remind me to be thankful. So many great things happen when you feel the thanks in your heart. I am incredibly grateful for every day that I wake up, for all my loved ones and for everything I have.

CHAPTER 11: ONLY IMPRESS YOURSELF WITH YOUR OWN DEFINITION OF SUCCESS

'Failure is success in progress'
Albert Einstein

Inner Lion

We could spend eternity worrying about what others
think, some comments unkind,
then realise some people just complain for the sake of
complaining you'll find,
I admire the lion crossing the road, trusting, walking
blind,
I unlocked a secret in life, the past we need not rewind
and keep playing it over and over in our mind,
In life we can beat ourselves up,
we must learn to live in the present in a half full cup,
let us trust in our decisions and not let influence take over
our inner guide,
let us be ourselves and let our inner lion shine,
just remember to take one step at a time
and try never to go back to catastrophising about what
others think,
you'll unlock greatness in life because it goes by in a
blink,
So be the lion of your own life and hear the calling in the
wild,
listen to your inner gut and release your inner child
where you didn't care what others thought
and freedom from fear was sought.

Success to everybody is different. Success, to me, is being able to get out of bed in the mornings, to remember to eat, to look after my self-care, to take my tablets every day and to raise my children the best I can. It is to never give up hope. It is to 'look back but not to stare' and take some lessons with me. Success to me is helping others find their own success. It's taking one step at a time, it is acceptance in others and ourselves, it is having peace of mind. I think success is finding the time to get to know yourself. It is bringing a smile to someone without looking for one back. It can be having belief in yourself and having confidence in your abilities. It is not focusing on your mistakes but telling yourself that you are worth it. Success is knowing that success is only a word that it is not to be compared to others but in being successful for yourself. For me, success is being well and when I'm unwell to believe that I am still successful if I just do one thing that day or don't do anything. Just recover...

CHAPTER 12: LIFE IS A MIRACLE - IMMERSE YOURSELF IN THE SPIRITUAL

'There are only two ways to live your life. One is as though nothing is a miracle the other is as though everything is a miracle'
Albert Einstein

One

One dream, one plan, one epiphany,
dreamt in stooges skies,
one life that vanishes like quicksand,
the endless earth abound in short supply.
One home, one universal kingdom,
upon which she seeks to knock,
her forlorn manner and depth of pain,
to which she cannot fake or block.
One door, one offered opportunity-
to enter she is scared,
she likes to stay inside her comfort zone,
in case her internal zombies are bared.
Many dreams, many plans, many epiphanies,
that she had always known,
yet One Life is all we have, to exist with or without,
a wild daffodil on her own.

I connect myself to the moment by trying to be aware of my surroundings and I can do this by saying to myself what can I see around me, what can I hear, what can I touch, what can I smell, what can I taste and what my intuition tells me. It's kind of like the 54321 skill I've mentioned already. This brings you back to the moment. You can set the scene while you do this, go into a room with little or no distractions, light candles, keep a hot water bottle beside you to relax you, put on music or nature sounds or open a window to hear the birds chirping while you relax if you like. I love looking at positive quotes with beautiful pictures, it makes me feel good. Looking through quotes online also helps me get to know myself better. I can see which ones I like and which ones I don't like. I like to share positive quotes on Facebook as well, it might just be relative to somebody else and it may just cheer them up, I hope.

I love going walking in nature, along the canal or beach, near a lake or in the mountains. It allows me to be at my best, forget any worries, just breathe in the moment. I love to see the smile on my children's face while we are exploring somewhere new. I love meeting new people and experiencing similar ideas or interests. I have some great friends whom I value dearly. I may not always see them but when we do meet it's like we never had time apart. Everyone that is part of my life is a beautiful wonder of the world. I love you all so very much. Life is so precious and short that it is good to live in the present and enjoy each moment instead of worrying about what has happened and what will happen. I am so glad I was able to stop worrying about the little things in life. It is good to make things happen and embrace change into your life instead of sitting back and waiting for things to happen. Get out of your comfort zone and attract the good things into your life now.

My miracles are my son and my daughter, they are my world. There were some complications when my children were born but thankfully they were ok. When I see them every morning, they are a reminder to me that miracles do happen and dreams do come true.

CHAPTER 13: ONE THOUGHT CAN ATTRACT A LOT

'If you think you can do a thing or think you can't do a thing you are right'
Henry Ford

Just One Thought

Just one thought alone can stay in our heads,
it makes us want to hibernate in our beds,
we've to try to fight this feeling with not just our meds,
but by catching those thoughts, letting them forever shed.

Let them fall to the ground, a burden you no longer wear,
bad thoughts in our mind can be harder to share,
it's negative self-talk that you've let take prominence,
instead write down many self-compliments.

Listening to music can help lift or change your mood,
getting proper sleep, eating healthier food,
or positive audio books or watching your favourite show,
all of these can impact your lives and your thinking flow.

Distract bad thoughts listening to your favourite song,
'*Fight Song*' is my favourite to put on,
write down in your diary a quote per day,
it's ok to say to yourself that you're feeling afraid.

When the worrying thoughts do come knocking,
don't give in, keep talking,
say to yourself that they will pass
and they will but you got to believe they won't last.

'Whenever you find yourself doubting how far you can go, just remember how far you have come. Remember everything you have faced, all the battles you have won and all the fears you have overcome.' (Daily Inspirational Quotes Facebook Page) If you change your track of thoughts for better ones instead of bad ones then you will, like a magnet, attract goodness to you. When you tell yourself you are going to lose then you automatically lose focus, you don't care as much and you quit and give up. See yourself winning, say it, think it, see it and it will happen.

I started practicing The Law of Attraction that was revealed in 'The Secret.' Everyone takes something different from a book but I do believe you can attract positive things into your life based on the ability to change your thoughts and actions. I am talking from experience over the last seventeen years. I started seeing and following different signs. I changed my thoughts, this wasn't an easy process but I started to feel better in myself, especially in my stomach, my head and my chest. I used to feel anxiety like a tight pain in my stomach and my chest.

I stopped complaining, (well it's a working progress). I started writing positive pieces and poems, I reduced my television time and replaced it by reading or listening to audio books. I thought of a few compliments for myself for every negative remark I had about myself. Everything that I've mentioned above can all have an impact on how you think. The bad thoughts never go away completely I don't think but you can choose which ones you listen to and which ones you send packing.

'New day…New thoughts…New strength…New possibilities…' (The Quantum Key to Abundance Facebook Page)

CHAPTER 14: YOU WILL ALWAYS COPE WHEN YOU HAVE HOPE

'H.O.P.E: hold on pain ends'
Unknown

Hope

You'll always cope
when you have hope,
a light in the dark found,
a guide through unknown ground.

Hope is the silver lining left in the sky
when the cloud passes by,
it is belief in yourself and others,
the fulfilment of your dreams discovered.

Hope is looking into your children's eyes,
it is found within the stars or deep within the ocean tides,
the laughter of the little ones gliding down the slides,
hope is persisting when life tries to capsize.

Hope can leave you vulnerable, hope can make you cry,
but better to say you were hopeful than to not even try,
hope is forever, hope is always there,
hope can be found through God when you say a prayer.

If you do at least one nice thing for someone then they may do something nice for you or someone else and it has a knock-on effect where helping is contagious. We all need hope to survive. Hope gives us the strength to carry on. Hope is a motivator. Hope makes dreams a reality. Wake up today and say I am going to make a difference to someone's life for the better. Let go of the past and don't worry about the future. Love yourself. Release your worries, if you have to, write them down. Feel them evaporate as they leave your shoulders and reach the page. Hope is a wish in your heart. Two inspirational people I am honoured to call my friends are both founders of two different charities but both so important and are changing people's lives in a positive way making an impact on individuals and on society. I wish them both the very best. They bring something very special to people - they bring hope. 'Hope can make the present moment less difficult to bear, if we believe that tomorrow will be better, we can bear a hardship today.' (Thich Nhat Hanh)

My beautiful friend Donna set up a charity called Neil's Hugs Foundation. They Help, Understand and Give Support to families and friends affected by suicide. Donna wrote the following piece:

'My name is Donna and I am the mum of one child his name is Neil, he is no longer on earth. He died on the 18th September 2011 age 32 from suicide but because he is not here it doesn't make me any less his mum. My son was my world and I did not know who I was anymore or what my place was anymore when I lost him. Grief never goes but somehow I manage to function day to day.

I knew when I found my strength, I would want to do something to try and make a difference to people who have been affected by suicide and raise awareness of what is happening in the world. I set up a charity called Neil's Hugs Foundation and we went live in 2017 with our first support group for families and friends who have lost someone to suicide. We have grown in the type of support we offer, providing safe spaces for people to go, 121 support and many other things.

61

We are building a community, all working together to improve poor mental health and reduce suicide levels locally. We have already been asked to help provide groups in other areas of Scotland and I can only see the need for organisations like ours to increase as we try to work together, supporting people who are struggling with poor mental health. Our charity is simple, we need a room, kettle and cake and we can offer people a safe place to talk. Please be kind to every person you meet in life, you never know what is going on in people's lives and your kindness might just make a difference to them. My name is Donna and I am Neil William Paterson's mum.'

Lorraine, another amazing friend of mine, is the co-founder of Our New Ears, and wrote the following piece:

'Our New Ears is a 100% voluntary organisation in affiliation with Chime, The National Association of the Deaf. It was formed quite accidentally in 2011 when, the Facebook page Anna's New Ears was set up to tell of one child's journey some parents connected. It was decided that they needed their own space and Our New Ears was formed. One of the parents, Denise McShane had the idea to put a sign up in Beaumont Cochlear Implant Department which turned out to be the key to the success of the page. It transpired that it wasn't just those parents who wanted to connect. The Happy New Ear Campaign of 2013 was made up of parents from this page, now many of whom were friends. It was successful in changing government policy in Ireland to provide 2 cochlear implants instead of 1 for all deaf children in Ireland.

Auditory verbal therapy (AVT) was next on their list. AVT is a proven specialist speech and language therapy for deaf children. With early diagnosis, correctly fitted technology and correct therapy they believe a deaf child can have age appropriate hearing by the time they start school. AVUK (Auditory Verbal UK) trained therapists in Ireland in their initial training. One went on to become a fully qualified AVT – Rosie Gardener.

Our New Ears is now known as ONE, but when we think back it was always the power of one. One child, one need to connect, one idea to post in one significant place. It has a different committee who are Rachel Broderick (a veteran member), Laura Keating and Ger McAuley who are

63

challenging perceptions all over again. They sit on every influential committee in Ireland and further afield. They have a voice and it is respected. The public Facebook page has over 4000 followers, but more importantly there are over 500 families of deaf children now connected in a safe, non-judgemental place, brought together with the same belief: there are no limits on our children.'

CHAPTER 15: YOU WILL BE ACCOMPLISHED IN MAKING COMPLIMENTS

'Talk to yourself like you would to someone you love'
Brené Brown

Smile

Be accomplished in making compliments no matter how you feel,
the goodness rubs off on you, and towards you the positivity will reel,
it will always come back around like a great revolving magic wheel,
have confidence in yourself and your true self you'll reveal.

Try compliment every person you meet, they're not hard to say,
it doesn't cost anything, give someone a smile without delay,
let them know you appreciate them in every way,
you never know you might just make someone's day.

Smiling is contagious you can pass it around,
otherwise, you'll be frowning, staring at the ground,
evoke your true self and confidence you will ooze,
try it, you've got nothing to lose.

Have you ever heard the number of times making a complaint to somebody multiplies? If you tell ten people then ten people tell their friends and it is contagious. Well, I find if you give someone a compliment you're passing on good vibes to that person as well and it may send a smile their way. When you feel low you tend to question every good remark. If you complain about people it's just negative energy hanging around that isn't needed. You are wasting your precious time moaning when in fact you could be making someone's day by giving them a compliment or doing them a good turn. If a person does you a bad turn try not holding onto any bitterness. You burn up energy complaining. The person that did the bad turn is taking up your energy if you let it burn inside you. Go directly to that person and ask why they did that; it could be that things got out of hand and the person may not have meant it.

Sometimes people act mean because that's all they've known since they were small. They might need a compliment even if they were nasty to you. They might just change their way if you bring out the best in them, their nicer side. They may even have had a bad day and they're taking it out on you. Remember, keep your cool and move on, it's a heavy load to carry if you're heaving bitterness around with you. Compliments are free. I would like you to think of at least ten compliments about yourself and write them down. I'll start you off with one: I am a determined person... Try to write out the full sentence not just the word because then it starts to sink in better and will have a positive effect on you. You could even write down 'because...' That will allow you to see the many different reasons you are wonderful. If you find this difficult, maybe ask a good friend to help, they will see many amazing traits you may not see. I've put a list of positive adjectives on the following pages to help you pick from and get you started:

Accepting	Enthusiastic	Organised
Active	Exciting	Original
Adventurous	Fair	Outgoing
Affectionate	Friendly	Patient
Ambitious	Funny	Peaceful
Appreciative	Generous	Pleasant
Artistic	Gentle	Protective
Assertive	Giving	Proud
Athletic	Gracious	Punctual

Authentic	Hard working	Quick-witted
Beautiful	Harmonious	Polite
Brave	Healthy	Positive
Calm	Helpful	Practical
Capable	Hilarious	Problem-solver
Carefree	Honest	Realistic
Careful	Honourable	Reflective
Caring	Hopeful	Relaxed
Cautious	Humble	Reliable

Charismatic	Idealistic	Reserved
Cheerful	Imaginative	Resourceful
Comfortable	Independent	Respectful
Compassionate	Inquisitive	Responsible
Confident	Interesting	Self-assured
Conscientious	Intuitive	Self-directed
Considerate	Inventive	Self-sufficient
Cooperative	Jolly	Sensitive
Courageous	Joyous	Sincere

Creative	Kind	Skilful
Curious	Knowledgeable	Spontaneous
Daring	Level-headed	Strong
Decisive	Light-hearted	Studious
Dedicated	Lively	Supportive
Dependable	Logical	Soulful
Determined	Lovely	Sympathetic
Disciplined	Loving	Talented
Dreamer	Loyal	Thorough

Dynamic	Merry	Thoughtful
Earnest	Modest	Timid
Earthy	Motivated	Trusting
Easy-going	Nature-loving	Trustworthy
Empathetic	Navigational	Understanding
Encouraging	Nurturing	Unique
Energetic	Observant	
Enterprising	Open-minded	
Entertaining	Optimist	

CHAPTER 16: IT'S NOT STRANGE TO EMBRACE CHANGE

'If life were a book then change is just the end of a chapter'
Unknown

Embrace Change

Try and step outside the norm,
it may just change your form,
try out something new,
a different view.

It may be good for you,
something different to do,
change allows for new things,
and excitement it brings.

It opens up new pathways,
it can be hard at first to adapt in the early days
but when you get into the swing
you can accomplish anything.

Get out of your comfort zone and do something that you would love to do. It may involve change that you may not be used to but you need to make that step towards doing something to move one step closer to your dream. Make that application for a course you'd love to do, apply for your dream job. If you're not in then you can't win! Volunteer. Ask your boss for that promotion you'd love. Make inquiries about the house that has just become available. Persistence is the key to unlocking the door of opportunity. Read a book that may just change your life for the better. Write the first chapter of the book you'd love to get published. Self-belief is vital, if you don't believe you can do it then how can anybody else. You need to look deep inside yourself and find yourself again. It is important to develop self-love as others will see what you see in yourself. If you see yourself in a negative way (I had many negative thoughts about myself) then it is harder for others to see the real you. Think to yourself: I am a beautiful person and your beauty will shine through for you and others to see. When you start to think positive and change your self-talk for the better you will attract positive people into your life like a magnet.

CHAPTER 17: KNOWLEDGE IS KEY TO THE FUTURE WE SEE

'The more we know the more we know we don't know'
Socrates

Journey

Every day I enjoy learning something new,
we are all just plodding through,
on this educational journey in life,
some are good moments, others carry strife.

We've just got to hold on and be grateful for every new dawn,
in a blink- things can go out of tune in our song,
but it's how we deal with these challenges that keep us strong,
try not to stress, our worries can be wrong.

Listen to others that have been there before,
they can put you on the right track that's for sure,
don't be afraid to ask questions to yourself and others,
discover the real you and all your wonders.

'Life is a circle of happiness, sadness, hard times and good times. If you are going through hard times have faith that good times are on their way.' (Thenetworkingweb.com) Every day is a learning experience. I love learning new things every day. I learn from my children. They are the best teachers. I enjoy reading and listening to self-help books. Reading 'The Magic of Thinking Big,' 'The Secret,' 'Chicken Soup for the Soul,' 'The Success Principles' 'You Can Heal your Life' and other books, I believe, unlocked something in my mind. Visualising and reviewing my goals helped me to achieve them. One thing seems to lead to something else. When one door closes another opens. Applying the principles to my life gave me the confidence to do things I would have never thought I'd do. I believe I thought myself out of depression, I thought myself well. These books gave me confidence to apply to college as a mature student where I never felt good enough to attend. I never gave it a second thought. I didn't give up when I didn't get in. I completed a further education course which was a stepping-stone to re-applying to college. Never give up!

CHAPTER 18: AFFIRMATIONS ARE MADE FROM OUR IMAGINATION

'Today is going to be a really good day'
Louise L. Hay

Affirmations

The sun is beaming through,
the morning has come, the day is new,
I can see all the different colours dancing around me,
yellow, purple, orange, blue, loads of colours I can see
little beads of dust floating in my view
they represent all the affirmations I wish to do,
each one takes their turn to catch my eye,
little seeds of dust flying by,
I can only see them in the light,
in darkness they are gone from sight,
I visualise each one that I want to do,
I make it my business for them to come true.

Affirmations are things you can say to yourself or write down to affirm something. You could make positive affirmations. For instance, you can say 'I am delighted I am making my goals come true' or 'I am happy now that I am a non-smoker' (even if you are trying to quit but still smoking) Write them down on a piece of paper or notebook. You could also write down the good qualities you have or wish to have. Keep writing down these affirmations and notice how clear your mind is. A heavy, cluttered mind can put you off track and divert your thoughts leading you down a negative road.

Louise L. Hay has helped me so much through her book 'You can Heal your Life' and through her YouTube videos. She has sadly passed away but still helps many people through her work. Jillz Guerin is a YouTube content creator that inspires me and motivates me to regain my confidence and embrace life in a more positive way.

If you clear your mind then you clear away any thoughts you don't wish to be there. A clear mind opens up a pathway for all those positive thoughts to make their way into your life. I have an app on my phone called 'my affirmations.' You can put who or what you are grateful for on it, your favourite quotes, your prayers, positive statements about yourself, your affirmations, your goals and dreams or anything you want. You can pick beautiful background pictures of nature or even add your own pictures. You could watch it in the mornings and evenings as a slideshow to relax you or cheer you up. I find it lessens my anxieties; it gives me a focus in life. You can even include an audio clip on it from your family and friends. Relaxation music plays in the background while you watch it. It allows me to feel more gratitude and just makes me feel happier in general.

CHAPTER 19: SINK LIKE A ROCK OR SWIM TO THE TOP

'Only a life lived for others is a life worthwhile'
Albert Einstein

My Philosophy

My philosophy, my love of wisdom…
I've always been a deep thinker sometimes staring at the sun,
for answers of the unknown I used to question why.
Now I see that everything is in the eye of the beholder,
for everyone's perception is different of what the top of the pyramid actually is.
Self-actualisation is something we supposedly never stop at,
we never really are content when we reach the top,
we strive to add another rung on to the ladder of success.
This ladder that we climb so high, and put each other and ourselves under stress,
to try to rush up its bars without enjoying the scenic view, and let our worry overtake,
instead, have faith in the structure and maker,
cause worry can weigh it down and change the structure of the ladder.
But even if the ladder is upright and structure perfect,
it doesn't even matter if it's leaning at the wrong wall,
because we'll get there sooner or later.
And in the end…it was never really about the ladder, or the wall, or the rungs or surround,
just the people who joined you on the ladder and who helped you up when you thought you would fall.

It's hard to stay positive when bad things happen. Getting things out on paper always helps me. This is the start of a new day, a new beginning and a new decade. I am hopeful for the future and know that although things don't always go your way, it's your reaction to it that helps lighten the load. Yes, things may seem grim at the moment but they can't always stay this way. Sometimes the most challenging treks of life lead us to the most magnificent destinations.

'You're so hard on yourself. But remember everybody has a chapter they don't read out loud. Take a moment. Sit back. Marvel at your life: at the mistakes that gave you wisdom, at the suffering that gave you strength. Despite everything, you still move forward. Be proud of this. Continue to endure. Continue to persevere. And remember, no matter how dark it gets, the sun will rise again.' (Lessonslearnedinlife.com)

Don't be afraid to avail of the many supports around you. There were many supports around when I fell ill and they all had a positive impact on contributing to my wellness.

Depression is a terrible thing and has destroyed so many lives. Some people can't live with it anymore and unfortunately their lives are tragically cut short. When I was twenty-one I was in a very dark hole myself and I didn't see a way out. I ended up in hospital. I am very grateful to still be here today.

CHAPTER 20: VISUALISATION LEADS TO INNOVATION

'Vision without execution is hallucination'
Thomas A. Edison

Visualise

Close your eyes,
breathe in and visualise-
go to your favourite place,
step outside life's race,
see yourself there in your mind,
breathe out the negativity-
it will help you unwind.

Believing is seeing. The great leaders of the past had a plan and visualised that plan before they finally created what they wanted to create. Martin Luther King Jr. made change happen because he could see it. He was a visionary leader who was deeply committed to accomplishing social justice through nonviolent means. 'I have a dream' was his famous speech. Make change happen for you.

Doing a mind map is a good idea to help visualise things. You could draw pictures or create your own vision board or life plan putting up pictures and words of all the things you want and wish to happen for you. Keep it somewhere you will see it every day. I created a vision board and hung it on my wall. I used mostly positive words and pictures to make mine. For the next one I used lots of Post-it notes and I divided it into three sections. 0-1 years, 2-5 years, 5 years plus and a completed section. You can use a large sheet of paper as the background. You could write down different categories. You can cut out words and pictures from magazines or you can print them off the internet. You can create your own vision board in a special book like a scrapbook or even on a board. You could write about what you want in your daily life, your hopes and dreams, aspirations and inspirations. I first heard about vision boards through John Assaraf in Rhonda Byrne's 'The Secret'.

I have a couple of vision boards on paper. Vision boards allow you to see on paper exactly what it is you want and create a picture in your head which seems to bring people that step closer to their dreams. I have one as my screensaver on my computer. It gets you thinking precisely what it is you want and allows you to see that picture in your mind every day. The greatest athletes use visualisation techniques to get where they want to be.

The following are different categories you could have on the vision board

- Family, loved ones, friends
- Gratitude
- Values/ character
- Strengths
- Love, marriage, relationships
- Health and fitness
- Interests and hobbies
- Household
- Social life, community, connections
- Career, work
- Financial, money
- Educational, wisdom, knowledge
- Adventure and travel
- Favourite quotes, poems, stories
- Mini goals
- Life dreams

Imagine you can and you will. Visualisation is a big part of success in life for a lot of people. I try taking each day one day at a time and I am more aware of who and what I have in life. Successful footballers use visualisation techniques to win matches. Many other goal-driven successful people use this technique. If you can see it in your mind then you're already halfway there. The most famous inventors used the power of visualisation to create. Keep looking up and know that if you fall you can get back up and try again and if you do look down, it's ok, you might just find something unusual like white feathers or a lucky penny. It is said when you see a robin, white feathers or butterflies it is a sign from heaven. It could be anything that you see in life that is a sign for you, you'll feel it in your gut or it will fall right into your hands or your life. When you get that feeling, know that you're on the right track and things can only get better.

Think about winning or completing these goals. Without goal setting how do you know you are on the track you wish to be on? Goal setting is so simple yet takes time and helps you get to know the real you. What is it you really want and when do you want it? Write down a list of goals and try to make them smart goals. Specific, Measurable, Attainable, Relevant and Timely. (George Doran, Arthur Miller, and James Cunningham)

Be specific- write down exactly what you wish to accomplish, who, what, where, when, how, track the progress and measure the result. Ask yourself are the goals linked with what you truly wish to achieve and is there a time limit on them? Grab life by the reins and live it to the fullest because we only get one and we may as well enjoy it while we can. There is positivity in everything we do, like the silver lining, we just have to dig deep and find it. Keep looking up for that rainbow and you'll find it! Know that if you fall you can get back up and try again. 'If it rains look for rainbows, if it's dark look for the stars' (Oscar Wilde)

Mistakes are there to be made and to show you that you are on the right track. How can you figure out the right way to do something if you don't make a mistake? If you are on a path that you don't think you should be on, there will be something good about that path that will lead you to new and exciting things.

CHAPTER 21: HAVE AN INQUISITIVE MIND AND LET GO OF YOUR PRIDE

'The man who asks a question is a fool for a minute, the man who does not ask is a fool for life'
Confucius

Inquisitive Minds

Why does the grass blow briskly in the breeze?
Why do the leaves in autumn shed from the trees?
Why do some people see flowers and others see weeds?
Why are the gigantic glaciers melting measurably overseas?
Why do those who are different sometimes get mocked and teased?
Why is there no cure for all disease?
Why is it good for us to eat our greens?
Why when we don't want something do, we say 'that's all we need'
Why is there mostly bad news in the articles we read?
Why does the whole world rotate at such soaring speed?
Why do the birds fly in the sky with such elegant ease?
Why is the key rack the last place we look for our keys?
Why is it so hard to walk tall in high heels?
Why do we close our eyes when we sneeze?
Why when we are sick do we splutter and wheeze?
Why oh why do we ask such questions as these?
Why? Because of our inquisitive minds indeed.

We can all be inquisitive as to when something will happen in our lives. When we will find true love, when we will find that dream job or when we will go on a fancy holiday? The answer to finding these dreams is within you, just delve into your inner consciousness and visualise dreams you hope to come true and in doing so you are allowing yourself to open up to new opportunities. The world is your oyster and everything you want can come true, you must have belief in yourself, believe that it will happen and it will. We learn in life by asking questions.

CHAPTER 22: LEARN FROM THOSE WHO LIFT YOUR LOWS

'Try to be a rainbow in someone's cloud'
Maya Angelou

Pay it Forward

People can impact you in a massive way,
it's more than just what they say,
to follow in their footsteps, you can strive,
it's what they do, they can change your life.
I have been influenced by many people indeed,
many books I've read, they plant a seed,
it develops in your mind and grows into a plant,
they say there's no such thing as 'I can't'.
They compliment you and say you can,
they believe in you, they GIVE A DAM,
they take you to the sun
when you were aiming for the moon,
they save your life, they hand you a spoon.
So pay it forward in all you do,
let them know they helped you get through,
I've even been impacted by lyrics of many a song,
they make you feel good and stay with you lifelong.

There are many people who have influenced me in my life. Many people have made an impact in my life and have had a big part to play in making a difference for the better. I love life and I am so grateful for my family and all those who are a part of my life. God has changed my life in a very special way. I feel at ease when I pray to God, then my worries are taken and I am filled with the amazing ingredients to improve my life: love, gratitude, peace, happiness, patience, perseverance and comfort. My family and friends have impacted my life in a very special way. Many authors have influenced my life in a very magical way although I have not had the pleasure of meeting some of them yet. I love their positive way of expressing their advice through their books. Rhonda Byrne's great Secret brings the power of gratitude to a whole new level. I listen to Jack Canfield's audio book 'The Success Principles' often and I find it helps keep me positive.

CHAPTER 23: IT WOULD BE A HELP TO BE YOURSELF

'Life isn't about finding yourself life is about creating yourself'
George Bernard Shaw

Silver Lining

She had a slip, she wasn't coping,
her mind racing, her heart broken,
she dreadfully missed her baby boy only four weeks old,
you'll be home soon she was told.

For so long she'd been feeling very low,
in the hospital time went by very slow,
it was bipolar she was diagnosed with,
felt like forever in there for a three-month stint.

But she found out she was not alone feeling this way,
she had needed this rest after been worn out most days,
since she was fourteen, always on the go,
she stopped to smell the roses all the time she didn't know.

She returned to college to complete a management degree,
and then completed the teaching HDip in FE,
she knows all the times she's had a breakdown,
has made her a stronger person all round.

She started a personal development course to keep her on track,
it helps build up your confidence to prevent a set-back,
she loves attending her writing group and enjoyed teaching computers,
she enjoyed doing the volunteer programme for literacy tutors.

She sees the positive aspect of her illness though,
she used to worry about the past, it sent her low,
she is glad she had more time to enjoy with family and friends,
and discover another part of herself where learning never ends.

She'll look out for the signs, that's for sure,
she will enjoy every moment that comes knocking on the positive door,
she is going to take every day as it comes, she has vowed,
there is always a silver lining on every cloud.

Everyone in this world is unique and different and never feel you should have to act any different around others, we're all human after all. I used to be influenced about what other people would want me to do and say and I'd act accordingly. Now I realise that I'm my own person and if somebody doesn't agree with what I have to say then I'm not going to lose sleep over it. We're all entitled to our own opinions. It's ok to agree to disagree. Be yourself, don't be afraid to get your views out there. If somebody doesn't agree or appreciate where you're coming from and it affects your friendship then you have to question if they really value you.

People can have clashes and arguments but if it is happening all the time you must nip it in the bud and explain to that person that you are not happy with how they are acting. Keep your distance from those who bring you down, if they want to be a part of your life then they won't act that way. I tell anybody constantly talking negatively that I have an invisible bubble around me and that anything negative they say is going to bounce right off me. Complaining about all different people and things will just start to bring you down. There's a difference if someone or someone's family member is in bad health or is going through a bad time, but sometimes people seem to like discussing the pitfalls of life.

CHAPTER 24: COME FORTH INTO A STATE OF COMFORT

'May time heal your heart and memories comfort your soul'
Unknown

Comfort

For children there's comfort in soothers, blankets and bears,
it's in our wisdom, we feel it in our prayers,
it's found in different places, even felt when one shares,
there's comfort in the eyes of everybody that cares.

Comfort comes in many varying forms,
it's the scent of roses without touching the thorns,
it can come to us in unknown ways,
it's that sense of completeness shining like the sun's rays.

Comfort is made in families, friends and unconditional love,
comfort is the softness of the feathers of a swan or a dove,
there's comfort in releasing our emotions,
we need it in our medicinal potions.

Comfort- This two-syllable short word is so much more,
it allows us to be at ease, a feeling one can't ignore,
it's in the joy and laughter of our loved ones,
for some, the sound of traffic or how a hummingbird hums.

Comfort can be felt against our skin,
it's warmth and softness soaks deep within,
it's in our own truth, it can be following our goals,
it's acceptance in ourselves that awakens our souls.

This poem is dedicated to my dear friend Teresa who passed away.

Think of what comfort is to you and keep those people or things close to you. It might be your family or friends, a favourite book or even photographs. In the Decider Skills course that I've mentioned already, they recommend that you create a comfort bag, like a soothe bag that you can take out whenever you are feeling down or out of sorts. These are potential things you could put in the bag: photos, your vision book, scented candles, hand cream, cards from loved ones, a sketchbook and pencil, favourite poems or quotes, letters or anything that comforts you. The course opens you up to more information on wellbeing and helps you to see you aren't alone with your illness and that you can be there for others as well.

There are many more supports available now for those who are suffering with mental health issues. The more you take part in these supports the stronger you will become. Life's fears and challenges won't seem as heavy when you get involved in these groups. One of the best decisions of my life was attending a personal development group for two years. It was filled with laughter and fun.

Today, thanks to everyone, my confidence has risen and I feel stronger. I feel it created a roadmap of wellness for me which then allowed me to start back on the HDip in Further Education. The support I received upon my educational journey was phenomenal. There were many supports available for me and I am thankful for this. It is good to open up about your illness and see that there are so many people rooting for you and trying to help you to get to where you want to be.

CHAPTER 25: NATURE TALKS GET OUT FOR SOME WALKS

'To walk in nature is to witness a thousand miracles'
Mary Davis

Lough Ennell

The reeds are gently swaying,
the rippled water circulates-
the trees, the lake they're framing,
the reflection of the sky and sun illuminates.

The dandelion swiftly passes by,
its seeds slowly dissipate,
you can't hear a pin drop nor a sigh,
it's presence echoes across the lake.

The swans and ducklings are resting at the shore,
there is tranquillity in the air,
they are on a mission to explore
but safety comes first as they take extra care.

Nature Talks

Trees are blowing, winds are light,
birds are encompassing, taking flight,
the rain is dribbling in drips and drops,
wondering and willing until it stops.

The baby birds squawk softly in their nest above,
I always love to see a beautiful robin or a dove,
robins remind me of loved ones deceased,
while doves have a spiritual meaning of peace.

Nature talks but are we listening,
quiet, hush, hear the whistling
of the wind above maybe talking to us,
what would it say, would it make a fuss?

One can relax to the sound of the gushing
bellowing forwards backwards and hushing,
the echo of the wind envelops everywhere,
it comes and goes but is always there.

Walk in nature. Breathing in nature can de-stress you and the beauty of nature can change any negative mindset into a positive one. Walking every day really helped me when I was at a low ebb. I really feel the fresh air and fitness helped me to get well. A walk or a cycle helps me to feel good especially if I'm with people I care about. Sometimes a walk on your own can be tranquillity to the mind, taking in nature and just enjoying the beauty of the world. Say to yourself 'I will look out for unusual things on the walk today.' I love seeing a robin on a walk, it reminds me of those dear to my heart that have passed on.

CHAPTER 26: GETTING THROUGH ANXIETY WILL OPEN UP VARIETY

'Life is ten percent what you experience and ninety percent how you respond to it'
Dorothy M. Neddermeyer

Tidal Tendencies

'Into the living sea of waking dreams', (John Clare)
dives imagination, all is not as it seems,
ebbing, flowing, forwards, back,
thoughts won't stop, racing - mind packed,
heart thumping, chest pain lingers,
body shaking, trembling fingers.
Deep and dark the ocean sways,
different colours, capturing sun's rays,
wild and raging, calm yet rippled,
medicine swallowed, musings trickled,
mind frozen, can breathe again,
count the breaths - one to ten,
normality again until the next time,
fighting battles against yourself is trying.

I've had bad anxiety in the past and have had to deal with some panic attacks. I was getting chest pain, feeling like it was heart related. I got the relevant checks and the doctors linked my chest pain to anxiety. It's a horrible thing. My medication is working along with natural self-help therapies like frequent doctor visits, listening to positive audio books and practicing gratitude. I enjoy looking at my affirmation slideshow with things I'm grateful for and my goals and dreams.

CHAPTER 27: THE SECRET WILL LAST WHEN YOU LET GO OF THE PAST

'You can't start the next chapter of your life if you keep re-reading the last one'
Michael McMillan

Seeds of Life

The wondrous days that pass,
with each swift breath blow fast,
the seeds of life are cast-
oblivious to how long they are actually going to last.
Those parading through the park,
each step a crunching footprint to my heart,
the lost tears wasted from the start,
unopened memories faded throughout my past.
Afraid of life but terrified of none,
constant worries weighing a tonne,
feeling lost, alone and tiresome
but eternally searching for the stars and the sun.
Feelings of hope and optimism in bundles,
sunlight radiating the unlimited tunnels,
rainbows glittering in the puddles,
distant are the worrying troubles.
Have I found what I was seeking for?
the stars cannot be found on the floor,
never had I unlocked the opportunity door,
happier now than I ever was before.

Dreams Searched...
Fear Forgotten...
Leaves Settled...

I have held onto the past for many years and I feel I've finally allowed myself to let go of it. What clicked with me was that I felt in order for me to release the past I had to stop blaming others for my mistakes I have made in life and take responsibility. I had to forgive. I had to forgive others but most of all I had to forgive myself. I had to forgive myself for people I felt I let down in life, especially my family and friends. I had to forgive myself for many things. I am truly sorry to anyone I hurt along my path. A void existed in me since I was little and I wanted to escape, run away. When I let go of the past I feel I released a lot of anger and resentment I carried on my shoulders. I still have work to do but feel a burden has been lifted.

Thinking of the past will only set you backwards. Forgive yourself for your past mistakes and try and move on. Continually dragging up the past for yourself and others only leads to a path of self-destruction. Know that mistakes are ok and they help you learn and grow. I wasted many days and nights worrying about the past. This caused me a huge amount of anxiety and stress. After I had my first breakdown, it took a while but I began to see things in a new light. A more beautiful light.

I try to take each day as it comes and try and forget the past and try not worry about the future. 'Whatever will be will be.' We can just try and live in the present moment and live each day with hope, love and meaning.

CHAPTER 28: THE BEST MEDICINE IS LAUGHTER AND PLENTY MORE AFTER

'My general attitude to life is to enjoy every minute of every day'
Richard Branson

Best Remedies

Try not to take life too seriously,
take risks deliriously,
laughing is good for the soul,
healing life's hurts, you've got to go with the flow.
Read a joke book or watch a comedy,
catching up with a friend can be the best remedy,
laugh till your tummies are sore,
travel to a place you've never been before.
Buy tickets for comedian shows,
read a funny book that will lift your lows,
learn to laugh at yourself,
laughter is great for your health,
play a sport or do an activity that you enjoy,
remove any stress from your life or just even try.
The best remedy is laughter,
Then plenty more after!

Why go through life so serious? Laughing is good for the soul. It releases natural, feel-good endorphins and is known to reduce stress. Watch a comedy movie or funny program, exchange jokes or funny stories or poems with family and friends, take your time and enjoy the beauty of life. We need to see what we can do to bring us back to our childhood and smile like we used to. Smiling reduces stress and it is contagious. These are things we can do to make us smile more. Join a sport or play a sport with your loved ones for fun. Read some funny quotes or jokes. Play games, even create your own ones. Define what fun is to you then just do it. You could write a list of things that make you happy and try and do more of what makes you happy.

My Happy List

- Chilling out with family
- Hearing my children laughing
- Looking at photos of my loved ones
- Family hugs
- Playing guitar
- Swimming
- Filling my positive jar
- Toasting marshmallows on a fire
- Chicken soup (the book and the soup)
- Movie night
- Writing poems
- Attending the writers' group
- Watching favourite programs
- Playing Disney movies
- Playing badminton
- Going to Zumba
- Making a snowman with the kids
- Surprising people
- Going to the beach
- Listening to Jack Canfield
- Camping
- Writing and illustrating stories with Lily
- Flying a kite
- Going to the zoo
- Carnivals
- Painting
- Sketching
- Cycling
- Creating a vision board or a scrapbook
- Looking at the stars
- Learning a new skill
- Going on holidays

CHAPTER 29: NOSTALGIC CHRISTMAS MAGIC

*'May you never be too grown up to search the skies on
Christmas Eve'*
Unknown

A Christmas Poem

Christmas is a time to be jolly,
you know it's close when you see all the lights and the
holly,
it's a time for family and friends to be together,
reminiscing on distant loved ones that are in our hearts
forever.
Mrs Claus is busy in the workshop with the help of all the
elves,
no presents are left unthought of, all ready to be sent from
the shelves,
this gives all the children, even adults, hope, awe and
delight,
Santa is in his sleigh, ready to take flight.
When he takes off, he has the most spectacular view,
he passes the sky and the moon too,
from the sleigh above, in the midst of the sky,
he brings presents and peace, swiftly meandering he does
fly.
The glittering snowflakes and the sparkles on the snow,
remind us of wonder and awe as Santa flies high and low,
Christmas crackers, candles, flashing lights and parties
too,
reuniting and rejoicing with family and friends old and
new.

I love Christmas. It's a time for family and loved ones where you can reunite. I love the sparkling lights, the hustle and bustle, the atmosphere in the shops, the Christmas music. I love listening to the Christmas albums on the record player, it brings back some childhood memories. I love to see the excitement in my children's eyes as it draws closer. I love to see their faces on Christmas morning. I look forward to watching Christmas movies with the kids for the month of December. I really enjoy buying gifts for family and friends. I love decorating the Christmas tree. I look forward to the traditional Christmas dinner with all the trimmings. It's really special for the children when it snows at Christmas. I still believe in the magic of Christmas.

CHAPTER 30: INNER GUIDANCE- A PATHWAY TO PEACE

'Peace comes from within. Do not seek it without'
Gautama Buddha.

Heaven's Golden Fleece

Reflections on oceans, rivers and lakes are deep, tranquil and intense,
when one can truly soak in these waters, life can absolutely make sense,
our thoughts can hold us back like a bound, barbed wire fence,
when we still our minds and reflect on the goodness it will raise our confidence.

Positivity can be the way forward, it's more than just a feeling,
when we see the things we hope to achieve then believing is truly seeing,
inner guidance leads our quest on this journey that connects hope and meaning,
the world of spirituality can be a guiding path of healing.

Stars of wonder and bewilderment disperse dreams, love and peace,
when we catch a glimpse of one then panic will undoubtedly cease,
our worries will abscond as we are enveloped in a golden fleece,
as heaven's cloth is beautiful, without a groove or crease.

Listen to your inner instinct inside and go with it. Follow the signs that are meant for you. Trust that you have both the knowledge and experience to make decisions that are the best for you. It is important to take time out for ourselves and meditate. Meditating doesn't necessarily mean deep breathing, although taking time out to do breathing exercises can be very effective to get you in a more relaxed state. Meditating can be listening to relaxing music, looking at photographs, making goals or exercising. Anything where you feel you are recharging your batteries, mindfully, physically and holistically. Be true to yourself and don't question following your inner gut. Sometimes it may look like you've gone off the beaten track but you may just be brought to an even better path. Try and make that quiet time for yourself. You are worth it.

When I fell ill it was far from peaceful in my head. I was trapped in my own head of unrealistic thoughts, fighting demons in my mind. I lost myself completely and I felt like I was someone else, a different person, whom I didn't know. I think it has a lot to do with past experiences of ordeals I had to deal with as a child that I never got help for. I was worrying about everything. I thought I'd never see the end. I can now say that I have peace in my own mind. Some days are more peaceful than others but I've learnt to manage this. I will list below things that allowed me to find this inner peace.

- Re-found Faith
- Family and friends supporting me
- Counselling
- Attending my writing group
- Volunteering
- Wellness Course
- Taking my medication
- Reading / listening to self-help books
- Meeting new people
- Writing affirmations and goals down
- Trying my best to think positive
- Stopped complaining (mostly)

CHAPTER 31: A FAMILY OF GEMS I'VE FOUND WITHIN THE NLN

'Family…A group experience of love and support'
Marianne Williamson

Turas

It was September 2016 when I started in Turas,
a group that has shown such strength and courage,
everyone that I've had the pleasure to meet and get to know,
my thanks I cannot begin to show.
You've made me feel like a part of something special,
you've lifted my confidence to another level,
I can always feel the warmth inside this class,
there's comedy and humour, I've had an absolute blast.
I'm honoured to have made friendships with all of you,
the hard times and lows you've helped me through,
this was an experience for me I'll always remember,
seems like a lifetime ago when I started that September.
It feels like I know you all for many more years than that,
I'm always here for you all if you ever need a chat,
you've all made my journey so wonderful and great,
in life you have restored my hope and faith.
We've shared many laughs, with some downs we've been hit,
you have inspired me with your generosity, strength and wit,
from the bottom of my heart I wanted to say,
thank you so much for being there for me in every way.

I am proud to have met such wonderful people on the wellness group I attended for two years. My confidence in myself has been lifted. My wellness has been the best it has been in a long time from attending this course and being a part of something great. I enjoyed the banter and the laughter everyone brought with them. I enjoyed finding myself again and finding friends that are like family to me. I enjoyed learning how to weave willow and learning how to crochet again. I loved the art and the tai chi. Through stress management I feel I am better able to deal with things. I love doing computers and I was delighted with the opportunity to volunteer teaching computers. I enjoyed going to the gym and going on outings with the group.

CHAPTER 32: SPRINKLES OF MAGIC WITH INKLINGS

'Infinite beauty, infinite adventure, infinite love – this is
the realm of creativity'
Laura Jaworski

Inklings

I am committed to writing my book,
of late I've had writers block feeling a little stuck,
the writers class gave me an inspirational push,
I've let other things take over, as such,
from this day forward I'm going to set time aside,
to focus on my book, it's now I must decide,
to make it priority and top of my list,
and realise that you have to work hard to reap the benefits.
If I could help others from reading my self-help guide,
it would make me so happy and fill me with pride,
I would love to have it published eventually,
and one day to become a best-selling author potentially,
no harm to have dreams and visualise,
in the hope that they can materialise,
I'm going to allow an hour every day,
to express thoughts and ideas that come my way,
so, in the here and now I'm making this step with
determination,
to bring me closer to my dream and aspiration,
I want to be the author of 'Seeds of Life and New
Beginnings',
and here's to everyone's dreams as well and all that it
brings,
a group that has brought a lot out of me, a great bunch
that have moved and inspired me so much,

the inspirational writers' group are called 'Inklings'
where one can write and talk about all different and random things,
no need to worry about whether you can or cannot write,
it just flows in the group and if it doesn't nobody is going to bite,
it's a trusting, warm environment where you can just be yourself,
some pieces are humorous, others are heartfelt,
it's not just about the writing though, I'd recommend even if you're feeling bleak,
my fellow Inklings are my friends that I have the pleasure of meeting each week.

I am a part of a remarkable writers' group. We are usually assigned a piece of writing per week after class. I wrote this piece above. The chosen heading was 'My commitment to a particular project.' I wrote on my commitment to writing my book. I also wrote a piece about Inklings and combined the two. I think because I have written this, it has since pushed me to allocate more time to continue writing my book. Although I haven't stuck to the time allocated, I have since put in more time. The writers group allows me to focus more and more on my writing and contribute more to the book. I really enjoy it and the writers never cease to amaze me with their outstanding masterpieces. I am so proud to be a part of everyone's writing journey as well. Those who are working on projects, those who have published or are awaiting publishing and those who are even just thinking of it in the future. Never give up.

CHAPTER 33: THE FUTURE BEAMS WHEN YOU FOLLOW YOUR DREAMS

'Dreams are like stars, you may never touch them, but if you follow them they will lead you to your destiny'

Liam James

The Right Direction

Follow the path to your dreams,
it will be easier than it seems,
write down your goals on a board
and mini action steps towards
finding out what you want so much,
it's within your grasp, just reach out and touch.
Explore create, grow and open that door,
it will help you get to know yourself much more,
the taste of freedom is nearer than you think,
believe in the good thoughts, the rest will make you sink.
I believe in magic and miracles too,
look out for the signs that are meant for you,
find things to do standing in that queue,
you'll always find something nice to think or do.
I try to just keep looking at the stars and the sky,
my perception is different, my spirits high,
I changed my outlook, the silver lining I can now see,
I feel more grateful for everyone, for everything, for life, for me.

It's never too late to follow your dreams in life no matter how old you feel, or how much energy you feel you lack or how sometimes people close to you might say you can't do it. It's not that they're intentionally saying the wrong thing, they may just be trying to protect you from getting a knock back. What they may not know are setbacks are good for you. Although they don't feel comfortable to us at first, the more we have them the more we become accustomed to them and the more they will drive us forward in the right direction. Each day we wake up I feel we have a new chance at life. A new dawn to make the most of. Let's dream big…why not?

Paradise

Hey, do you know what Paradise is?

To me it is seeing loved ones again that I dearly miss,
when loved ones give me a hug and a kiss,
the special memories I cherish about which I reminisce,
when I saw and held my children for the first time it was
absolute bliss.

It is pain-free and peaceful in paradise,
it is having fun with my children, maybe flying a kite,
it's the warmth of the sun on my face, the temperature just
right,
It is roasting marshmallows with loved ones on a campsite.

Paradise to me is a relaxing atmosphere,
it's travelling the world with loved ones, trying to get away
once a year,
it's that feeling of resilience having nothing to fear,
it's the excitement coming up to Christmas, indulging in
the festive cheer.

Paradise is spending time with the ones I love,
it is seeing a robin nearby or even a dove,
seeing rainbows, sunsets, shooting stars in the night sky
above,
paradise is the good days when life fits like a glove.